EARTH SCIENCE—OUR PLANET **Need to Know**

Water on Earth

by D. R. Faust

Consultant: Jordan Stoleru, Science Educator

Minneapolis, Minnesota

Credits

Cover and title page, © yyuuuyu/Shutterstock; 3, © desertsolitaire/Adobe Stock; 4–5, © Tomas Maracek/iStock; 6–7, © Public Domain/NASA; 8–9, © icemanphotos/Shutterstock; 10, © Kit Leong/Shutterstock; 11, © Marina Va/Shutterstock; 12–13, © Rasto SK/Shutterstock; 15A, © icemanphotos/Shutterstock; 15B, © AlinaMD/Shutterstock; 15C, © ND700/Shutterstock; 15D, © Creative Travel Projects/Shutterstock; 16, © Damsea/Shutterstock; 17, © Yalcin Sonat/Shutterstock; 19, © Evgeny_V/Shutterstock; 21T, © Cacio Murilo/Shutterstock; 21B, © Bilanol/iStock; 23, © Dennis MacDonald/Shutterstock; 24, © Elizaveta Galitckaia/Shutterstock; 25, © Lasse Johansson/Shutterstock; 27, © simonkr/iStock; 28, © ArtMari/Shutterstock.

Bearport Publishing Company Product Development Team

Publisher: Jen Jenson; Director of Product Development: Spencer Brinker; Editorial Director: Allison Juda; Editor: Cole Nelson; Editor: Tiana Tran; Production Editor: Naomi Reich; Art Director: Kim Jones; Designer: Kayla Eggert; Designer: Steve Scheluchin; Production Specialist: Owen Hamlin

Statement on Usage of Generative Artificial Intelligence

Bearport Publishing remains committed to publishing high-quality nonfiction books. Therefore, we restrict the use of generative AI to ensure accuracy of all text and visual components pertaining to a book's subject. See BearportPublishing.com for details.

Library of Congress Cataloging-in-Publication Data

Names: Faust, D. R., author.
Title: Water on Earth / by D.R. Faust.
Description: Minneapolis, Minnesota : Bearport Publishing Company, 2026. |
   Series: Earth science-our planet : need to know | Includes
   bibliographical references and index. | Audience term: juvenile
Identifiers: LCCN 2025005925 (print) | LCCN 2025005926 (ebook) | ISBN
   9798895770719 (library binding) | ISBN 9798895775189 (paperback) | ISBN
   9798895771884 (ebook)
Subjects: LCSH: Water–Juvenile literature. | Hydrologic cycle–Juvenile
   literature.
Classification: LCC GB662.3 .F38 2026 (print) | LCC GB662.3 (ebook) | DDC
   553.7–dc23
LC record available at https://lccn.loc.gov/2025005925
LC ebook record available at https://lccn.loc.gov/2025005926

Copyright © 2026 Bearport Publishing Company. All rights reserved. No part of this publication may be reproduced in whole or in part, stored in any retrieval system, or transmitted in any form or by any means, electronic, mechanical, photocopying, recording, or otherwise, without written permission from the publisher. Bearport Publishing is a division of FlutterBee Education Group.

For more information, write to Bearport Publishing, 3500 American Blvd W, Suite 150, Bloomington, MN 55431.

Contents

A Day at the Beach 4

The Blue Planet 6

Feeling Fresh 10

Around It Goes 12

Wonderful Water 16

Too Little, Too Much 20

Water Worries 22

Keeping It Clean 26

The Water Cycle 28

SilverTips for Success 29

Glossary 30

Read More 31

Learn More Online 31

Index 32

About the Author 32

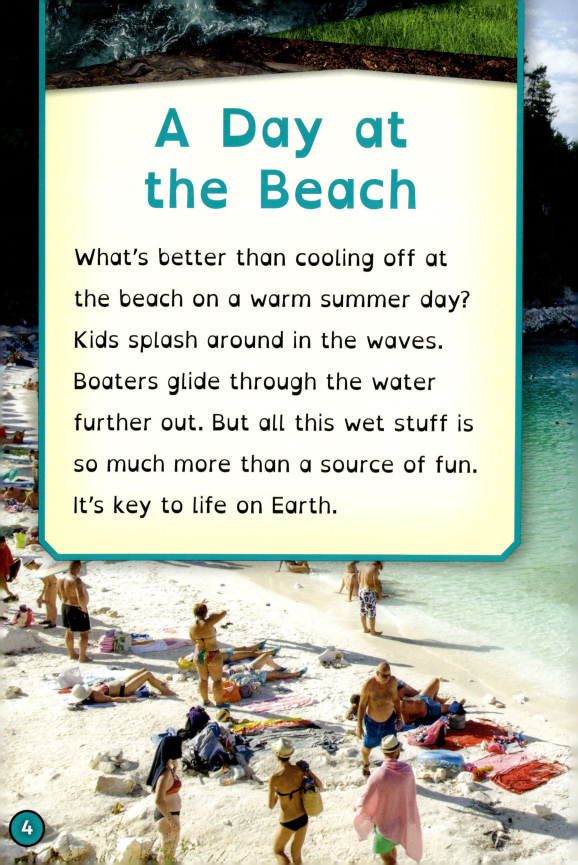

A Day at the Beach

What's better than cooling off at the beach on a warm summer day? Kids splash around in the waves. Boaters glide through the water further out. But all this wet stuff is so much more than a source of fun. It's key to life on Earth.

Humans have a long history with water. The earliest societies around the world formed near water. Many were built up along rivers and lakes.

The Blue Planet

Earth is sometimes called the Blue Planet. This colorful name comes from all the water on its surface. About 71 percent of the planet is covered with water. It flows in rivers and streams. Large amounts of it collect in lakes and the ocean.

There is also frozen water on Earth. Most of it can be found in ice sheets. The largest of these thick layers of ice and snow are near the poles.

About 97 percent of Earth's water is salt water found in the ocean. There are five named oceans on Earth. We use these names to make the water easier to understand and study. However, all the oceans are actually one large, connected body of water.

How does the ocean get salty? Salt is found in rocks on land. When it rains, some of this salt is washed into waterways. Over time, it collects in the ocean.

Earth's Oceans

The Atlantic, Pacific, and Indian Oceans are Earth's major oceans.

Feeling Fresh

Most of the water on land is not salty. Rivers and streams are moving bodies of fresh water. These **landforms** flow because of **gravity**. The force pulls water downhill.

Eventually, this fresh water collects in ponds and lakes. Some of it flows into the ocean.

Some rivers and streams go into human-made lakes. People create these lakes to store fresh water. Then, the water can be used by homes and businesses nearby.

Around It Goes

The amount of water on Earth stays mostly the same. But the liquid does move and change in the water cycle. It travels between the ground, air, and ocean over time. At different points of the cycle, water is in different **states**, or forms.

Only a small amount of Earth's water is moving in the water cycle at one time. Most of it is stored somewhere. It can be found in the ocean, clouds, and ice.

Heat turns liquid water on Earth into **vapor**. In this gas form, water rises. It comes together in clouds. As clouds get full, they let out the water. Sometimes, it falls to the ground as rain. Some of it comes down as snow, which eventually melts. Then, the cycle starts again.

Earth's water moves through this cycle over and over. In fact, some of the water that is in you right now may have once been a part of a dinosaur!

Wonderful Water

Liquid water is what makes life on Earth possible. All living things need it to survive. Many animals drink fresh water. Most can go only a few days without it.

Plants use water to make the energy they need to grow. Farmers often water the crops we will later eat.

Bodies of water are home to many different plants and animals. Scientists believe between 50 and 80 percent of all life on Earth is found in the ocean.

People have found ways to use water for more than just survival. We swim for fun and travel around the world in boats.

Water can also be turned into energy. Moving water pushes the blades of a **turbine** that makes power.

Because the water cycle is never-ending, power from water can be, too. This makes it a **renewable** source of energy.

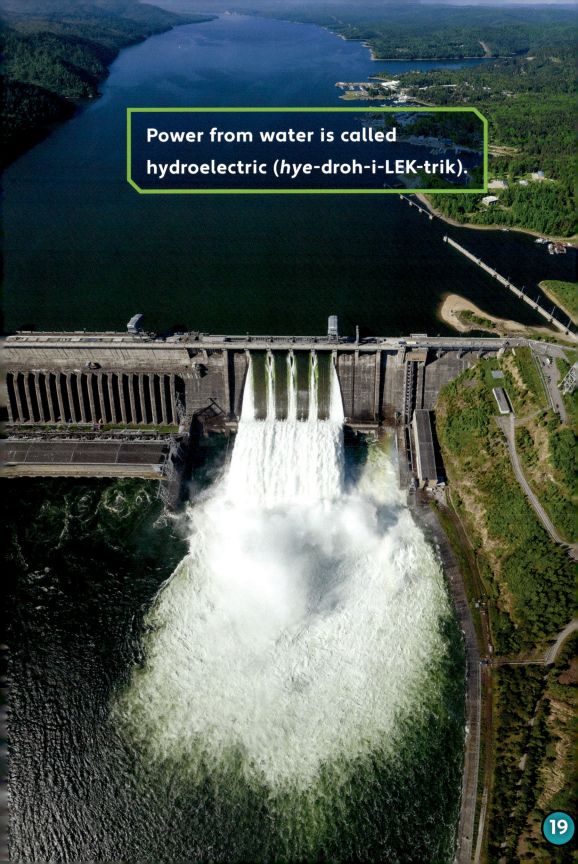

Power from water is called hydroelectric (*hye*-droh-i-LEK-trik).

Too Little, Too Much

We need water. If an area doesn't get enough rain, it may go into a **drought**. Wet landforms could dry up.

However, too much water can also be a problem. If it rains too much in a short time, rivers and streams can flood. They cover nearby land in water.

> Droughts can lead to wildfires. These dangerous fires are more likely to start in areas that are very dry. They burn faster and hotter when fueled by dry plants.

Water Worries

Unfortunately, harmful weather is becoming more common. This is because Earth is getting hotter. Earth's **climate**, or the typical weather, is changing with this heat. And that impacts the planet's water. It is leading to more rain in some places. At the same time, it is making droughts last longer in others.

Greenhouse gases keep Earth warm. Like the walls of a greenhouse, they trap in heat. Humans add more of these gases to the air when they burn **fossil fuels** for energy. This is warming our planet.

Many factories get power by burning fossil fuels.

A warmer Earth also means more melting ice and snow. A lot of the planet's water found in these solid states is melting. All this water needs to go somewhere. It ends up in the ocean. As the ocean rises, land along the coasts floods.

> More liquid water is turning to vapor as Earth warms. The gas collects in clouds full of water. This leads to stronger rainstorms. When these storms form over the ocean, they can become **hurricanes**.

As ice melts, animals that rely on it are put at risk.

Keeping It Clean

We couldn't have life on Earth without water. Luckily, there's a lot we can do to help our watery world. Keep the planet's water free from trash and chemicals. Use less energy to stop Earth from heating up. Let's work together to keep the blue planet healthy.

> One of the easiest ways to help Earth's water is to use less. Turn off the tap while you brush your teeth. Take shorter showers.

The Water Cycle

The water cycle keeps our wet world going.

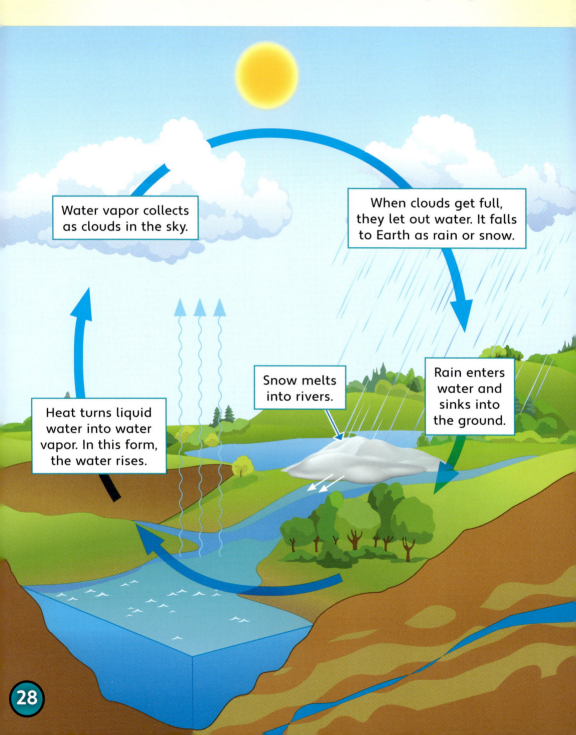

SilverTips for SUCCESS

★ SilverTips for REVIEW

Review what you've learned. Use the text to help you.

Define key terms

drought
flood
fresh water
salt water
water cycle

Check for understanding

Name some of the differences between bodies of salt water and fresh water.

Describe the steps of the water cycle.

What are the different ways humans use water?

Think deeper

How would your life be different if Earth's water changed dramatically?

★ SilverTips on TEST-TAKING

- **Make a study plan.** Ask your teacher what the test is going to cover. Then, set aside time to study a little bit every day.

- **Read all the questions carefully.** Be sure you know what is being asked.

- **Skip any questions** you don't know how to answer right away. Mark them and come back later if you have time.

Glossary

climate patterns of weather over a long period of time

drought a long period of time when there is very little or no rain

fossil fuels energy sources such as gas, oil, and coal that are formed from the remains of animals and plants that died millions of years ago

gravity a force that pulls objects toward one another

greenhouse gases the gases that trap heat around Earth

hurricanes powerful storms with heavy rain and fast winds that form over large bodies of water

landforms natural features on Earth's surface

renewable able to be replaced by a natural process in a short period of time

states ways or forms of being

turbine a large fan that spins when air or water flows past it

vapor something in the form of a gas

Read More

Emminizer, Theresa. *The Water Cycle (Nature's Cycles in Review).* Buffalo, NY: Enslow, 2024.

Kuehl, Ashley. *Lakes and Oceans (Earth Science-Landforms: Need to Know).* Minneapolis: Bearport Publishing, 2025.

Vale, Jenna. *Floods: The Worst in History (World's Worst Disasters).* New York: Gareth Stevens, 2025.

Learn More Online

1. Go to **FactSurfer.com** or scan the QR code below.
2. Enter "**Water on Earth**" into the search box.
3. Click on the cover of this book to see a list of websites.

Index

climate 22
drought 20, 22
energy 16, 18, 22, 26
flood 20, 24
fresh water 10, 16
gravity 10
greenhouse gases 22
ice 6, 12, 24–25
ocean 6, 8–10, 12, 16, 24
rain 8, 14, 20, 22, 28
salt water 8
streams 6, 10, 20
water cycle 12, 18, 28

About the Author

D. R. Faust is a freelance writer of fiction and nonfiction. They live in Queens, NY.